SIMPLIFY THE SEASON

SIMPLIFY THE SEASON

Rediscover Christmas Through Advent

ERIN OLSON

XULON **PRESS**

Xulon Press Elite
2301 Lucien Way #415
Maitland, FL 32751
407.339.4217
www.xulonpress.com

Printed in the United States of America.
Edited by Xulon Press.

ISBN: 9781545610497

ENDORSEMENTS

In a world increasing with noise and busyness, Erin Olson's new devotional, *Simplify the Season*, gives the reader permission to pause during the Christmas season and focus on what truly matters. The journey from Hope to Revelation reminds us of the reason for this season. The best Christmas gift is Jesus, and this devotional will help you remember this once again.

Dave Phillips
President and Founder,
Children's Hunger Fund

Our culture writhes in a frenetic whirlwind of noise and confusion. We need hope. We need quiet. We need clarity. In her new book, *Simplify the Season*, my friend Erin Olson has given us a beautiful tool that will help us all on the journey to reclaim a hope-filled, peaceful inner life during the Advent season.

Michael Neale
National Best-Selling Author,
Lead Worship Pastor,
Prestonwood Baptist Church

Simplify the Season is a beautiful read for anyone who believes and loves to celebrate the birth of Jesus. Erin Olson writes simple but profound, short but eloquent. I enjoy the way she reminds you of old Truths in such a new and refreshing way; it's as if you had never heard it before. Truly a gifted teacher! Each daily reading will leave you hungry for the next time you read it. You won't be disappointed. A concentrate of Advent joy!

Rev. Jennifer E. Ryerson
Associate Pastor,
First United Methodist Church
(Springdale, Arkansas)

TABLE OF CONTENTS

ACKNOWLEDGMENTS

J ESUS, THANK YOU for leaving the comforts of heaven to come to this earth, live, and die a horrible death for me.

Thank you to my husband, Scott, for his unconditional support and love.

Thank you to my children, Spenser, Grace, and William, who cheer me on in their own special ways.

Thank you to my mom and her husband for believing in me and supporting the work God has called me to do.

Thank you to all my co-laborers who so diligently work the harvest.

ABOUT THE BOOK

MORE THAN TWO thousand years ago, the only Son of God departed heaven and became flesh. The world anticipated the coming Savior, but when He finally arrived, the people waited and looked for something different and better. We live similar lives today.

Through the pages of Scripture, the world has experienced the birth, death, and resurrection of Jesus. However, every Christmas season, we run at a frantic pace to keep up with the demands of the season instead of simplifying the season to meditate on the anticipation, patience, hope, and revelation of Christ. We need to look back to the past and acknowledge His life and the fact He died for all the sins of the world. We must also look forward with patience, hope, and revelation to His second coming because every single day brings us closer to His glorious return.

Simplify the season this year by making time for your Savior. He is the reason for the season, and He is the One to be celebrated and worshiped. When we make a choice to simplify, we make room in our hearts and lives for His presence. May this simple Advent devotional help you as you pursue Him.

Each week, we will look at an aspect of the Advent: Anticipation, Patience, Hope, and Revelation. At the beginning of every week, there will be an activity, some questions to discuss / reflect upon, and a short prayer. My prayer for you is that at the end of this Advent season, you will have a better understanding of the simple life of Christ and the simple lives we are called to lead when we abide in Him and remain focused on His purpose for our lives.

Heaven kissed the earth for you!

INTRODUCTION

I NEVER IMAGINED THESE words would come out of my mouth, but I'm kind of a Christmas Scrooge. For as long as I can remember, I have loved Christmas. Sure, I went through years of pouting because I didn't get everything I wanted for Christmas, but I've always loved Christmas—until recently. I'm not sure if my attitude toward Christmas has changed because, well, we have so much stuff, or because I am more in love with Jesus these days and the things of this world just don't do it for me anymore. I'm guessing it's a combination of both.

I still put up my Christmas trees, sparkly lights, and do the Christmas shopping thing, but mostly I crave sweet time with my Savior as I sit in the glow of the Christmas lights. I want to discover more about who He is, what believing in Him means—both for the here and now and my future—and what His second coming is going to be like.

Amidst the busyness of the Western Christmas season, I am making a commitment to simplify the season. Since you are still reading, I pray you'll join me and rediscover Christ this Advent season through the pages of this devotional. I can't wait to hear all the testimonies that will come.

ANTICIPATION

A S YOU START out each week this Advent season, either by yourself or with a group of family or friends, light a candle, and:

Reflect on the following:

1. Do you remember what it was like before you personally knew Christ in your life? What did your life look like?
2. What is the most important thing you are anticipating this Christmas season?

Pray:

Lord, thank you so much for what you willingly gave up so many years ago so that I, along with every other person in this world, have the opportunity to receive the free gift of eternal life by believing in you. I pray you will fill me this season with awe and wonder, not only about your life, but about what you are still doing each and every day. May I get to know you even more this Advent. In Jesus' name I pray, amen.

DAY ONE

THE POSSIBILITIES

ARE YOU ALREADY exhausted, and the holiday season has not even fully ramped up yet? For many, last week included travel, cooking, family, football, and for the brave ones, Black Friday shopping. Although we paused momentarily to give thanks, a lot of people ran themselves ragged. If we are not careful, the next thirty days will test our limits. I think that's why I long to celebrate a purer Advent season.

In my house, I start the countdown to my birthday at least a month out. It is not that I do anything exciting on my birthday or even ask for that many gifts, but I just love my birthday. I don't spend a lot of time reflecting on my birth per se, but rather I spend some time reflecting on the previous year—perhaps even the decade I am leaving behind—but mostly, I reflect on the possibilities of the year ahead. Most people celebrate the milestones. For instance, if someone is turning sixteen, we do not celebrate just the birth of that sixteen-year-old; we

3

celebrate the fact that girl or boy is turning sixteen and all that sixteen entails. For those celebrating the big four-zero, we celebrate that milestone as well, and so on.

We get this right regarding our birthdays; however, during Christmas, Christians spend a lot of time focusing on the Christ baby in the manger. Yes, Jesus was born in a stable more than two thousand years ago and died on a cross, but He is also coming again (Revelation 1:7). While it is right and good to reflect on the miraculous birth of the Savior, we must also celebrate the possibilities of the coming year. For every year we celebrate His birthday, we are also one moment closer to seeing His return.

Let's make a promise to try to simplify the season this year and focus on the One who is, was, and is to come (Revelation 1:8). We do not have to exhaust and bankrupt ourselves both physically and financially. Let's not be so focused on Christmas that we miss Christ. As we dig through Scripture together and rediscover the **Anticipation**, the **Patience**, the **Hope**, and the **Revelation** of Christ, may each of you find a renewed peace in His presence.

FROM THE BEGINNING

HAVE YOU EVER met a person whose life appeared to be laid out entirely in front of them even before they were born? You know, the kind of person whose parents thought long and hard about their child before conception, picked out a name, placed them on a waiting list for the best preschool, predetermined the college they would attend, and, in some cases, declared what profession their child will have?

If this describes you, take heart; there is a person whose Father also laid out His life. His name is Jesus—the One who is—and He existed before all creation, and God had a plan for Him all along. That plan is redemption. From the beginning, God declared the seed of the woman would bring salvation to all, and this seed would be the only thing who would crush the enemy.

"And I will put enmity between you and the woman, and between your offspring and hers; he will crush your head, and you will strike his heel." (Genesis 3:15)

Christ's love and grace are woven throughout each of the eight sections of the Bible—the Law, History, Poetry, Prophecy, Gospels, Acts, Epistles, and Revelation. Does the fact that salvation has always been a part of the plan for your life change the way you feel about and view Jesus? How about when you think of His plan for your worst enemy or your most cherished loved one(s)?

As promises about Jesus in the Old Testament are revealed through the reading of God's Word this season, may you feel the **anticipation** of the promised Savior, and may the promise of salvation shape your Advent season this year in a fresh way.

DAY THREE

A FATHER'S OBEDIENCE

THE OTHER DAY, my younger son and I talked about some friends of ours who lost their young son several years ago to cancer. I mentioned there was someone else who knew a thing or two about losing a son. He knew to whom I referred, but it still didn't help the matter. He was visibly shaken by the fact that even though God can use all things for good, someone had to lose a child. He said he didn't think he would ever be okay if he had to go through losing a child. I love his tender heart, and at the root of it all, I am not sure any one of us would honestly be willing to lose a child—even if great good could come from it.

Maybe that's why I am even more grateful for the obedience of one man more than four thousand years ago. If someone tells you that God does not test your faithfulness or obedience, please tell that person he or she is wrong. God does, in fact, test us at times.

When Abraham was still Abram, God promised to make him into a great nation and make him famous (Genesis 12:3). However, just twenty chapters later, the Bible says, "Some time later, God tested Abraham" (Genesis 22:1). This was no pop quiz! It was the test of all tests. God told Abraham to take his son Isaac—the one whom he loved so much—to Moriah and sacrifice him as a burnt offering (Genesis 22:2). God tested Abraham by not only asking him to give up the thing he loved so much, but also to see if he would believe God even though it appeared God went against His covenant promise.

Would Abraham walk in obedience and push the limits of his logic and knowledge of God?

Yes, he would; and yes, he did.

Abraham packed up his son, some servants, supplies, and headed to the mountain. He responded to God's *"Go!"* by going, just as he had done when God told him to leave his native land and go to the land He was going to show him (Genesis 12:1).

Why was Abraham so willing to be obedient even though there was a tremendous cost? Because God had been faithful to Abraham. God had provided for him in that foreign land, and God had kept his promise by allowing Sarah to conceive and give birth to Isaac at an old age.

What took place in Genesis 22:3–14 was a glimpse of all Jesus would fulfill through His death. Although God stepped in and provided a ram instead of Isaac, God noted Abraham's obedience. God confirmed His covenant promise and told Abraham:

> I will surely bless you and make your descen-
> dants as numerous as the stars in the sky and
> as the sand on the seashore. Your descendants
> will take possession of the cities of their ene-
> mies, and through your offspring all nations
> on earth will be blessed, because you have
> obeyed me. (Genesis 22:17–18)

I am thankful for Abraham's obedience, and I am also thankful for God's faithfulness. God repeatedly remained faithful to Abraham and his descendants because it was God's plan (Genesis 18:18–19). God spoke a promise, and His promises are always true. The seed of Abraham became the seed of Isaac, which then became the seed of Jacob, and ultimately Christ was born out of that seed. The lineage of this seed consists of more than thirty families—more than half of which existed after King David—with whom the covenant promise was repeated (2 Samuel 7:12). That is a lot of years of waiting for the promise called Shiloh (Genesis 49:10).

Abraham's obedience has an impact on each of our lives today. His obedience and God's faithfulness overwhelm me when I take the time to recognize what they both did for me, for you, and for all future generations. God has not moved or changed, and His promise was just as true then as it is now. Sadly despite this, we often move through life ignoring the reason for our existence: to bring glory to God.

What greater act of obedience is there than to submit ourselves to the Father who sacrificed His Son for our eternal salvation? Abraham was confident God would provide "a sheep for the burnt offering" (Genesis 22:8), but put yourself in his place as he waited with **anticipation** to see how God would provide. Are you waiting on God's future provision in the second coming of Jesus with this same confidence?

DAY FOUR

HIS REDEEMER LIVES

CHRISTMAS IS A hard season for many people. It can be a reminder of loved ones who are no longer with us, the what-could-have-been or the fear of having nothing to provide for your children. These are things not originally meant to be a part of Christmas. As much as some try to fight against it, the season can send people into a depression they do not experience the rest of the year.

Job understood loss, depression, and sickness. God allowed Satan to interrupt Job's life. Job lost everything—his children, his servants, his riches, and his animals. He eventually became sick and lost the respect of his community. We do not know exactly how long Satan afflicted him. Some scholars agree it was many months, but less than a year. Satan said Job was righteous only because God had put a hedge of protection around him and that if God removed it, Job would become less than righteous (Job 1:10–11).

Even though Satan stretched Job almost as thin as a man could get, Job was relentless in his righteousness—even when his friends and wife encouraged him to curse the Lord and said the Lord had cursed Job for an unrighteous act. As Job lay in his depressed, sick state, he uttered these words:

"I know that my redeemer lives, and that in the end he will stand on the earth." (Job 19:25)

Even before the coming and advent of Christ, Job proclaimed he *knew* his Redeemer lives. He was full of **anticipation** that there was something better to come, that his Redeemer was one of strength—because of His coming posture—and Job had great comfort in knowing that despite all that would happen to him on this earth, he would one day see God (Job 19:26). C.H. Spurgeon once said this while preaching a memorial service:

"Dear friends, dear friends, can all of you say, 'I know that my Redeemer liveth?' The question is simple and simply put; but oh, what solemn things hang upon your answer, 'Is it MY Redeemer?'"[1]

It is not enough to say, "Jesus is *the* Redeemer." One must be able to say, "Jesus is *my* Redeemer." Job made it through his ordeal because he had heart knowledge of God *and* his coming Redeemer. Unlike Job, we have the testimony of Jesus' first coming. Like Job, we must proclaim the living Redeemer

---

[1] "I Know That My Redeemer Liveth by C. H. Spurgeon," Blue Letter Bible, accessed June 07, 2017, https://www.blueletterbible.org/Comm/spurgeon_charles/sermons/0504.cfm?a=455025.

as our own as we wait with **anticipation** for His advent. Do you? Will you?

If Jesus is the reason for the season, He is also the reason you can make it through this season regardless of what you are going through.

DO NOT BREAK THE FETTER

A S FAR BACK as I can remember, I have had a nativity scene (sometimes more than one) in my house at Christmas. Last year, I finally got my first outdoor nativity scene. When my son and I left the place where we purchased it, I said, "For sure we cannot ever move to a place with a homeowners' association because they may not allow us to put it in our front yard." He gave me a perplexed look.

In the news, the Christmas political correctness has already started. Even today I read about a state university sending out a request that campus parties not emphasize religion and culture or be "a Christmas party in disguise." I am sure it will only be a matter of days before the news will be talking about some person who is asking a town to remove their nativity scene from the courthouse or city hall. It happens every year.

Sadly, none of this should catch us by surprise. The psalmist in Psalm chapter two refers to kings and nations conspiring and plotting against and trying to free themselves from God, and His Anointed One (Psalm 2:1–2).

The psalmist goes on to vividly portray how God feels about this sort of behavior (Psalm 2:4–6). I'll let you read the specific words he uses, but let's just say God does not look upon this sort of behavior favorably.

I am certain God doesn't care whether I display a nativity scene at my house at Christmas, or whether the city puts one on display. However, God does care about our hearts, our motives, and ultimately His plan. As outlined in several places in Scripture, Christ has a specific purpose to fulfill—He will rule the world with an everlasting scepter.

"You will break them with a rod of iron; you will dash them to pieces like pottery." (Psalm 2:9)

Although many believe God doesn't exist, isn't at work, or doesn't care because bad things are happening in this world, He warned us—the entire world—in advance about the consequences of conspiring to plot against the things of God. He said:

> Therefore, you kings, be wise; be warned, you rulers of the earth. Serve the Lord with fear and celebrate his rule with trembling. Kiss his son, or he will be angry and your way will lead to your destruction, for his wrath can flare up in a moment. Blessed are all who take refuge in him. (Psalm 2:10–12)

I know pondering the wrath of God is not very Christmas-y, but the seriousness and **anticipation** of the Messiah were known long before His first coming, and it becomes more pressing as our world tries to break itself of Him. So, this season, ask yourself this question, "Has my Christmas lost its focus on the king God installed on Zion?" (Psalm 2:6). Use this time—these days—to secure the fetter.

DAY SIX

GOD IS WITH US

CHRISTMAS IS THE only time of year I enjoy getting the mail. I love the day the first Christmas card arrives in our mailbox. Each day, I quickly flip through the bills and junk mail, and I slowly open each card. I enjoy seeing the faces of so many friends and family members, as well as reading some of the handwritten notes. Indeed, the day after the last Christmas card arrives is a sad day for me.

On the cards, many put a word of inspiration or Scripture. So often, Isaiah 7:14 is quoted:

"Therefore the Lord himself will give you a sign: The virgin will conceive and give birth to a son, and will call him Immanuel."

The name Immanuel means "God with us." Names were important during the time the prophet Isaiah delivered this prophecy. For instance, the Lord told Isaiah to take one of his children, Shear-Jashub, with him to meet with King Ahaz (Isaiah 7:3). The name Shear-Jashub means "a remnant will return." Later in chapter eight, Isaiah's wife bears a son, and that chapter says the Lord told Isaiah to call him Maher-shalal-hash-baz, which means "swift to plunder and quick to carry away" (Isaiah 8:3). One of his sons had a name of hope, and one of his sons had a name representing God's judgment. That was a tough family dynamic, and would certainly serve as a daily reminder of both God's mercy and His power.

While the virgin giving birth to a son called Immanuel paints a serene image in our minds—one worthy enough to put next to our darling, innocent children on a Christmas card—this prophecy came at a volatile time. The wicked King Ahaz ruled during this time, and he was fearful of the kings of Syria and Israel who plotted against him. Although King Ahaz was in the lineage of King David, he refused to trust the Lord. His fear led him to seek help from the evil Assyrians.

The Lord told Isaiah that even though His care for the people of Judah was like gently flowing waters, the people rejected Him (Isaiah 8:6). The people of Judah needed only to fear the Lord. Instead, they chose to allow their fear and lack of trust to become a stumbling block. The king led the people so far away from God they lost sight of His majesty and forgot His promise of protection.

Scripture records Isaiah's response to the people. He said he would "wait for the Lord ... I will put my hope in Him" (Isaiah 8:17). As I mentioned earlier, names have meaning, and the name Isaiah means "Yahweh is salvation." Isaiah knew without a doubt that salvation was from the Lord alone. Isaiah's counsel, unlike his ungodly contemporaries, spoke of the coming Light and the need for the people to trust in the Lord. Today, our **anticipation** looks a little different than Isaiah's. We have access to the salvation Isaiah referred to through our faith in Jesus. We now wait on His second coming. This, too, gives us much hope.

Do the words Isaiah spoke about his source of hope flow freely from your lips?

DAY SEVEN

HE WILL BE CALLED

It IS NOT unusual for people to wait with great **anticipation** for an election year. If the person who is in office is not highly regarded, people are looking forward to having someone that might do a better job. If the person in office is highly regarded, people hold their breath to see who might win the election. It is also during election years we see, even with checks and balances, how a leader can shape a nation—for better or for worse.

When things are going well, people tend to care less. However, when things are going badly, people tend to see the dark side of things in living color—the darkness becomes even darker. Darkness allows a person to see their vulnerability and their need. For light to shine brightly, it must be shined into darkness.

It had been many months since Isaiah initially spoke of the virgin birth of Immanuel (Isaiah 7:14), and yet Isaiah still delivered the same message to the people—destruction and hope. The Lord, as He does so often, kept calling and warning His people through the prophet Isaiah, and each time the description of the Messiah was stronger and stronger.

"For to us a child is born, to us a son is given, and the government will be on his shoulders. And he will be called Wonderful Counselor, Mighty God, Everlasting Father, Prince of Peace." (Isaiah 9:6)

Isaiah told the people that this child would be the one in total control and that every nation, king, and person would bow to Him. Not only would this child be in control, but He would take care of the whole world, not just a certain aspect of it. This child would be unlike any other, and this child would grow up to be both king and priest, and bring with Him a rule of justice and righteousness that would never end.

Wonderful Counselor – God's wisdom

Mighty God – affirmation of the Messiah's divine nature

Everlasting Father – the Father's care continues forever

Prince of Peace – a leader who brings peace

Even as we focus on our political leaders, let us not take our eyes off the leader above all leaders—Jesus. Imagine for a moment what it must have been like for the people of Judah who, under the rule of a wicked king, were being led further and further into darkness, and yet God continued to passionately commit to utilize His heavenly armies to rescue His people (Isaiah 9:7). As dark as things might have looked, God sent Isaiah to tell them to **anticipate** the coming Light.

If you are honest with yourself, do you feel all alone and scared in the darkness—even though people may be around you? Read Isaiah chapter eleven and reflect on the promise God made to send out a branch from King David's line. The remnant consisted of the broken and the exiled—which is all of us. Wait with wonder as His story continues to unfold.

PATIENCE

A S YOU START out each week this Advent season, either by yourself or with a group of family or friends, light a candle, and:

Reflect on the following:

1. What is Jesus asking you to wait upon?
2. Are you rushing this Christmas season? Why?

Pray:

Lord, I know your timing is perfect. Forgive me when I try to move ahead of you and get impatient in my waiting. You left heaven in God's perfect timing. Everything about your life was prophetically announced and accomplished according to God's plan. Please help me see that despite how busy I am or how fast this world is moving, I am to always wait upon you. In Jesus' name I pray, amen.

DAY EIGHT

TIMING

H AS THIS FIRST week of Advent flown by for you? Honestly, I am slowly beginning to realize this year how busy I am during the Christmas season—even as I try to write this devotional and be intentional about my focus on simplifying the season. There are so many things that distract me—decorating, shopping, planning, children's school activities, family tradition outings, addressing hundreds of Christmas cards, and Hallmark Channel Christmas movies (boy, can they suck you in!). Days are short, hours are precious, and impatience runs high.

As I stop and reflect today on patience, I am reminded of the number of prophecies fulfilled in the person of Jesus Christ (over 350). These prophecies took a long time to fulfill. Nevertheless, what the Lord spoke to the prophet Isaiah was true—"At just the right time, I will respond to you" (Isaiah 49:8, NLT). It has, and will always be, about God's perfect timing.

Praise Him that one of the attributes of the fruit of the Spirit is patience (Galatians 5:22). He knew His people would need to be patient in the waiting of His fulfillment. We need patience today as we await His final fulfillment.

Do not rush today. Make an intentional effort to evaluate your life through the lens of His saving grace. This may include removing some things that interfere with you being able to truly appreciate and simplify your Advent season so you can focus more on Him, His promises, and the **patience** He is asking of us all.

DAY NINE

THINK BEYOND YOURSELF

E VERY YEAR AS I decorate, the branches of my Christmas trees and garland tear up my hands and arms. Sometimes it looks like I got into a fight with a sharp-clawed cat. However, just as quickly as they appear, they are gone—usually within a week or two. I try not to get the open wounds near dirt, and I try not to pick at the scabs. Occasionally, a deep scratch will leave a scar.

What happens when we don't give ourselves time to heal an open wound? We so often get in our own way, and sometimes, it creates a whole new set of problems. I am always amazed at the wonders of our bodies and God's precision and timing in how our skin can regrow itself and heal. It is simply amazing.

Injuries can also cause pain. Some injuries have little pain while others can be excruciatingly painful. Some people suffer in silence, and others have support systems. Some people are stoic and show no emotion, and others cry a lot. I think God made some of us more apt to cry and wear emotions on our sleeves. We need all people to make the Kingdom go around!

The prophet Jeremiah was known as the "Weeping Prophet." He allowed us to see his heart as he struggled to obey and see the emotional and spiritual battle he faced in delivering God's messages to the people of Judah. He is so much like me. While I do not like evil or wickedness, I have great empathy for people who find themselves in desperate situations. As much as I want people to "do the time if you do the crime," I also want them to heal and be made whole. Maybe that's why my children say I am a "crier." The world deeply troubles my soul.

God called Jeremiah to be a prophet when he was in his mid-twenties, but Jeremiah did not believe he was worthy or strong enough for what God asked him to do. God wanted Jeremiah to think beyond himself and realize the importance of the task at hand. God would provide and protect Jeremiah, but Jeremiah needed to be willing. Jeremiah was afraid of looking foolish—like any respectable young man might be—but it would have been much more foolish for Jeremiah to refuse to do what God told him to do.

Jeremiah would not have been what we classify these days as a successful evangelist. Only a few repented in his time, and Jeremiah struggled with the Lord telling him to *"Go!"* when all he wanted to do was remain peaceful with his neighbors. The irony is that peacefulness had become less and less, and as the time of destruction and captivity got closer, chaos abounded.

Jeremiah desired peace, and peace was the message he was to proclaim to the people. Jeremiah prophesied about the descendant the Lord would raise up from the line of King David, and proclaimed in that day, Judah would be saved (Jeremiah 23:5–6). Jeremiah prophesied the peace he desired.

Jeremiah prophesied of the new covenant with the people of Israel and Judah (Jeremiah 31:31), and the difference between the old covenant (external and legal) and the new covenant (vital and person-to-person relationship) (Jeremiah 31:33). The Lord repeatedly told Jeremiah, "The day is coming," but God did not tell Jeremiah when. If you know anyone with an emotional heart, the waiting is often the hardest part. Anxiousness riddled Jeremiah. God made some lofty promises—He would no longer tear down, but build up (Jeremiah 31:28), people would no longer be responsible for the sins of their parents, but would instead be personally responsible (Jeremiah 31:29), the new covenant mentioned earlier would be established, and Jerusalem would be rebuilt (Jeremiah 31:38).

Jeremiah prophesied to the people of Judah for more than forty years about the impending destruction and their need to repent and seek God. His soul was burdened for so long. He was an emotional guy, and his **patience** must have run thin. Jeremiah lived to see the destruction of Jerusalem and the Babylonian exile, but he did not live to see the good promises God told him to prophesy about.

God needed Jeremiah to think beyond himself for the sake of future generations—including our generation. The words Jeremiah had written in the scrolls were for people to hear throughout the ages until the coming of the new age. So, the question is, *Are you a person willing to think beyond yourself for the sake of others even if you do not ever benefit? Are you truly okay with witnessing finished works in heaven?*

Challenge yourself this season to discover what is important in your Christmas schedule. Is there anything eternal and intentional—maybe even a little uncomfortable? There is so much more still to come. Will you remain **patient**, faithful, and fully engaged? I hope so.

DAY TEN

HE RESPONDS WHEN HE IS READY

LOVED THE FIRST day of December as a little girl. My mom always bought me a cardboard Advent calendar. I could hardly wait every morning to open the corresponding number to see the chocolate shape hidden beneath the flap. It was nearly impossible not to open every number at once.

For the past few years, I have tried to do something special for my children during Advent. Several years back, I purchased a wooden Advent calendar with cute little doors on it that opened and had just enough space to put a small something inside. The problem is I have three children and only one calendar, so it was always a challenge to find three unique things that fit into the small compartments for twenty-five straight days. The first year, they loved it, but after a couple of years they got bored with it, and I got frustrated.

A few weeks ago, I noticed the cardboard Advent calendars at the grocery store checkout. Since I am trying to simplify the season this year, I picked up three of them. December first, I set them out for my children and waited for them to come downstairs. Seriously, who doesn't enjoy a little chocolate first thing in the morning? It has been fun to watch them not miss a day in opening their Advent calendars. They want to know what shape is behind the number, and more than once my youngest has mentioned how "he just wants to open every door right now because he just can't wait!" Time and **patience** are so related yet so diabolically opposed. It is hard for us to wait, whether we are waiting for big things or little things.

I wonder how the prophet Ezekiel handled the waiting? Ezekiel was thirty years old when he received a message from the Lord close to six hundred years before the birth of Christ. Ezekiel was a priest, but because he was living in exile in Babylon, he couldn't perform his traditional priestly duties (Ezekiel 1:1–3). The fact God would send a message to a priest living in exile was huge for the exiles because it showed them that God had not forgotten about them after all.

Time and again, the Lord gave messages to Ezekiel. Like his prophetic predecessors, the messages reiterated the people's rejection of God and His ways. Two times God specifically mentioned that He refused to listen to His rebellious people (Ezekiel 14:3, 20:3). However, God's messages were always laced with glimpses of His promise of rescue and restoration.

"And when I bring you back, people will say, 'This former wasteland is now like the Garden of Eden! The abandoned and

ruined cities now have strong walls and are filled with people!'"
(Ezekiel 36:35, NLT)

For close to six hundred years, God's people had to wait
for the One who is and was to come—six hundred years!
Generations died in the waiting. It is easy for us to look at the
people who lived during Jesus' time and say, "How could they
have missed it?" They had become hardened and skeptical in
their waiting even as God promised the following:

> I will make a covenant of peace with them; it
> will be an everlasting covenant. I will establish
> them and increase their numbers, and I will put
> my sanctuary among them forever. My dwelling
> place will be with them; I will be their God, and
> they will be my people. Then the nations will
> know that I the Lord make Israel holy, when
> my sanctuary is among them forever. (Ezekiel
> 37:26–28)

How are our hearts and attitudes any different today? God
fulfilled His promise to dwell among His people (Immanuel—
God with us), and yet our impatience runs high as we await the
complete fulfillment of Jesus' mission. We return to chasing
idols and completely distorting the meaning of Christmas. We
want "it" all now—whatever that "it" is—and ignore the fact
God works on His own time schedule.

Give yourself the gift of time and **patience** this season. Yield to His timing in *all* things—your schedule, your commitments, your plans, your expectations, and your future. Even if it means only getting one chocolate per day, He desires only the best for you in His due time.

DAY ELEVEN

HE DOESN'T MIND OUR QUESTIONS

D URING AN OFFICE Christmas party on December 2, 2015, a man and his wife opened fire on his former colleagues. The motive behind the shooting was linked to terrorism. The day after the attack, the *New York Daily News* printed this on its front page:

"God Isn't Fixing This"[2]

Social media and media outlets swarmed with comments about this statement, as well as the fact the *New York Daily News* mocked Republicans who offered heartfelt prayers for the families and victims of the shooting. As is often the case, superficial quick fixes are the desire of the people. In this case,

---

[2] Rich Schapiro, "GOP offers prayers, not solutions, on Calif. massacre," NY Daily News, December 02, 2015, accessed June 07, 2017, http://www.nydailynews.com/news/politics/gop-candidates-call-prayers-calf-massacre-article-1.2453261.

instead of addressing the deeper issue of rampant wickedness, gun-control laws became front and center.

Will God fix this issue? Have you asked Him?

God doesn't mind when we approach him with a sincere heart and ask Him questions. The prophet Habakkuk knew this. In just three short chapters, Habakkuk's conversations with God about the evils in Judah are written on the pages. The difference in the way in which Habakkuk questioned God and the way in which the *New York Daily News* questioned God are night and day. Habakkuk personally knew the God he was speaking about.

Read through Habakkuk chapter one and you will see how perplexed Habakkuk was. I am sure many people on the afternoon of December 2, and every day since, mumbled similar words to God. Even in our home this Christmas season, we are feeling a sense of uneasiness. There appears to be something different this Christmas season, and that difference is the spirit of wickedness. While we struggle with this issue, we also must come to terms with the fact the *New York Daily News* might be on to something. It might look like "God Isn't Fixing *This*" (emphasis mine) in our eyes because His plan usually looks a lot different than ours.

After Habakkuk spoke his complaints, the Lord responded:

"Look at the nations and watch—and be utterly amazed. For I am going to do something in your days that you would not believe, even if you were told." (Habakkuk 1:5)

God told Habakkuk He would raise up the wicked Babylonians to destroy the people of Judah because of their wickedness against the Lord. As you can imagine, this confused Habakkuk. The fact God would choose to use wicked people to punish His people did not sound right or fair to Habakkuk. Honestly, it doesn't sound fair to me either.

I know most of us would rather go into a temporary fairy-tale land during the Christmas season an

d forget all our troubles. However, the world keeps ticking in front of us. A lot of what we do at Christmas—the lights, the pageants, the food, the festivities, the shopping—is man-made. Life doesn't pause during the days of Advent.

Habakkuk decided to climb up on his watchtower, stand guard at his post, and wait to see what the Lord would say next (Habakkuk 2:1). The Lord replied and told Habakkuk he needed to write down the Lord's response on tablets so that it could be correctly carried to others (Habakkuk 2:2).

"This vision is for a future time. It describes the end, and it will be fulfilled. If it seems slow in coming, wait patiently, for it will surely take place. It will not be delayed." (Habakkuk 2:3, NLT)

Habakkuk responded to all he heard through prayer. He praised God for all that He had done for His people, and he pledged to wait patiently (Habakkuk 3:16). Habakkuk would not live to see the destruction caused by the Babylonians. Even when all looked bad and hopeless, Habakkuk declared, "I will rejoice in the Lord, I will be joyful in God my Savior" (Habakkuk 3:18).

The salvation, hope, and strength the Lord gives us are what we need to focus on this season. I know it is hard with so many distractions, but it is our lifeline to peace in our communities and in our families. In times of confusion and chaos, we need to retreat to our Savior and focus on what is important—even if what is going on doesn't make sense.

Climb up in your watchtowers this Advent, stand guard, and wait **patiently** for His promises to unfold.

DAY TWELVE

UNDERSTANDING TIME

C HRISTMAS LIGHTS WILL flat out test your patience. Our outdoor Christmas lights create problems every year. If it rains or if the sprinklers run, the lights short out, and inevitably something else in our house turns off because of the short. Inside the house isn't much better. Every year I say I am going to fix some of the burned-out bulbs, but every year I forget, and as we put up the trees, the tedious task of replacing and testing the bulbs is too much. I usually don't replace all of them because I run out of patience. I leave the burned-out bulbs for the following year.

Time is funny. What might only take an hour today will be put off for some time in the future. In the short term, it sounds like a good idea, but sooner or later, I am going to have to face the fixing of the Christmas lights. Even if I get a completely new pre-lit tree, the lights will eventually burn out as well.

Time sounds like it should be an easy concept to grasp, but that is not always the case—especially when someone is telling you things at lightning speed. I've been in those conversations before—the ones where you can't always tell whether the person is talking about something that has happened, is going to happen, or might not ever happen.

Zechariah got a message from the Lord with a timing issue. It is interesting that in one verse, the first coming of Jesus Christ is being spoken about, and then, in the next verse, His second coming is mentioned. It is no wonder people were so confused. If you only heard one part of the message but not the other, you might be looking for a coming king up above instead of right in front of you riding on a donkey.

> Rejoice greatly, Daughter Zion! Shout, Daughter Jerusalem! See, your king comes to you, righteous and victorious, lowly and riding on a donkey, on a colt, the foal of a donkey. I will take away the chariots from Ephraim and the warhorses from Jerusalem, and the battle bow will be broken. He will proclaim peace to the nations. His rule will extend from sea to sea and from the River to the ends of the earth. Then the LORD will appear over them; his arrow will flash like lightning. The Sovereign LORD will sound the trumpet. (Zechariah 9:9–10, 14)

God desires for us to be firm in our belief and trust in Him. Sometimes Bible verses are super-confusing, and like my Christmas lights, we tuck them away to deal with later. However, His Word is important. It gives us clues about what has happened and will happen. Zechariah, as both a prophet and a priest, encouraged those who had returned from exile not to do the same things that led them into exile in the first place. He gave them glimpses into the future work of Christ, but he told the people to remain focused on Him and to be patient in their waiting.

How often do we hear something that is promising and desirable, and then launch headfirst into trying to make it happen in our own strength? I know I tend to do that a lot more than I would like to admit. God, as He rebuilt the Temple, had a plan that was still five hundred years in the making. He only asked that His people keep doing the right things—be obedient and stay focused on Him. What He asked of them then is the same He asks of us today. His plan may require the **patience** of five hundred years, but it will be more than worth the wait.

DAY THIRTEEN

MANY SILENT NIGHTS

THE CLASSIC CHRISTMAS song "Silent Night" evokes images of the newborn baby Jesus' birth. However, before this beautiful, silent night took place, the Israelites faced many silent nights. No doubt, these silent nights left many people waiting impatiently for the Lord's promises.

The last words of the Old Testament are found in the book of Malachi. Malachi was a pastor, theologian, prophet, and a spiritual mentor. He truly had a multifaceted ministry and was dealing with many personalities. He cared deeply for the people he was reaching, and the book of Malachi begins and ends with a word of encouragement (Malachi 1:2, 4:2). In just four chapters, Malachi delivers six messages. In Malachi 3:1 the Lord said,

"I will send my messenger, who will prepare the way before me. Then suddenly the Lord you are seeking will come to his temple; the messenger of the covenant, whom you desire, will come."

For approximately four hundred years after the book of Malachi, God was silent. This period is known as the "Intertestamental Period." There are no recorded prophetic words in Scripture during this time (none of the writings written during this period were accepted as Scripture). The exiles were back in the land of Judah, lived under six different governments during this period, and their thinking underwent significant changes due to cultural influences.

Throughout the Old Testament, God promised to send a Savior—a priestly king—who would reign forever. How would you have reacted for those four hundred years? I can imagine every time a baby boy was born, people must have whispered, "Could this be the messenger to whom the Lord referred?" Oh, how their patience was tested.

The infamous Silent Night we sing about now is because of God's relentless love, mercy, and grace. God blessed two faithful, praying people willing to be used by Him to be a part of preparing the way for the Messiah. Zechariah and Elizabeth understood long suffering. Elizabeth was barren, and they were both old. One day during Zechariah's Temple duties, an angel appeared to him and told him Elizabeth would become pregnant and give birth to the one who would be the Lord's messenger (Luke 1:17).

I hope you caught that. Despite his circumstances, Zechariah worked unto the Lord. He wasn't completely checked out, nor had he given up—he was still involved in the work the Lord had called him to do.

I believe God gave Zechariah and Elizabeth years of silence to prepare them for the task ahead. God needed faithful, faith-filled parents who feared the Lord to raise the man who would fulfill this prophecy. God entrusted these two people with an important part in His plan. Their **patience** in the waiting and silence was tested. So is ours as we await the Advent.

The Christmas season has become anything but silent. There are days I crave silence, but often if I'm able to catch a few minutes of it, I don't know what to do with myself. I know that if I can't find silence, I have a hard time hearing from the Lord and preparing myself for the message or task He is trying to give me. I know I am not alone in this search for silence. God chose the stillness of the night—when all was calm—to make His earthly entrance.

Challenge yourself this season to find moments of silence. How long has it been since you sat in silence—not speaking, writing, or praying—waiting on God's next move or instruction?

DAY FOURTEEN

KEEPING A SECRET

I REMEMBER WHEN I found out I was pregnant with my first child. Once the initial surprise was over, and I had told my husband, I wanted to tell everyone I knew. However, most people tell a newly pregnant woman to hold off telling anyone the good news until the first trimester is over. Not sharing this good news was hard the first time, second time, third time, and fourth time. I didn't make it to the twelve-week mark on any of my pregnancies.

Zechariah, as we learned yesterday, received a visit from the angel Gabriel, who told him that he and his wife, Elizabeth, were going to have a baby. Because he and his wife were old, he was obviously shocked, and he questioned the angel. He said, "How can I be sure this will happen?" (Luke 1:18). That was not the response the angel was looking for, and he replied to Zechariah,

> I stand in the presence of God, and I have been
> sent to speak to you and to tell you this good

news. And now you will be silent and not able
to speak until the day this happens, because you
did not believe my words, which will come true
at their appointed time. (Luke 1:19–20)

Poor Zechariah lost his ability to speak. Shortly after that,
Elizabeth became pregnant, and she went into seclusion for
five months (Luke 1:24). No one knows why Elizabeth went
into seclusion, because it was not a custom or a command for
a woman to do this. She told no one about her pregnancy. I
just can't imagine becoming pregnant after years and years of
praying for a child, having a husband who came home from
his Temple duties unable to speak, and being holed up for five
months. Can you imagine the conversations Elizabeth had with
God during those five months?

The angel Gabriel also made a visit to Elizabeth's cousin,
Mary. He told Mary that Elizabeth was six months pregnant
(Luke 1:36). Mary responded in faith to the angel. Zechariah
could have learned from his younger relative, Mary. A few days
later, Mary made the four-day journey to visit Elizabeth. As soon
as Mary entered Elizabeth's home with an "Elizabeth, I am here"
greeting, the baby inside Elizabeth's womb leapt, and Elizabeth
was filled with the Holy Spirit (Luke 1:41).

Picture this—Zechariah is sitting in the house, unable to
speak, eyes wide open, watching all this unfold. Zechariah must
have been recalling his visit from the angel Gabriel who said the
baby "will be filled with the Holy Spirit, even before he is born"
(Luke 1:15). At the same time he recalled this, Elizabeth said to

Mary, "Why am I so favored, that the mother of my Lord should come to me?" (Luke 1:43). Talk about a "wow" moment.

When it was time for Elizabeth to give birth, she had a son. As is usually the case, people had lots of opinions and advice for the new parents. Many suggested Elizabeth and Zechariah name their son after Zechariah. However, the new parents knew exactly what the baby's name would be. Since Zechariah still couldn't speak, he wrote the name "John" on a tablet. The Bible says, "Immediately his mouth was opened and his tongue set free, and he began to speak, praising God" (Luke 1:64). His obedience displayed his faith, and he regained the ability to speak. Everyone instantly knew something special had taken place (Luke 65–66).

Holding this secret for nine months must have been difficult. It required immense faith, obedience, and patience by Zechariah and Elizabeth. They had great news to share, but the Lord wanted to protect Elizabeth and her baby. Sometimes good things don't happen immediately.

Everyone knows how hard it is to wait for a gift. My children start their Christmas lists months before Christmas. God made us wait for His gift. Christmas is the perfect time to share the gift of the true Christmas story. As Christians, we are called to share the Good News. For those who have loved ones who have not received God's eternal gift of salvation—even though you have shared and prayed—let's pray this Christmas they receive it. It is simply better than any gift you could buy or make for someone. May God reward your faithfulness, obedience, prayers, and **patience** as you participate in His plan.

HOPE

A S YOU START out each week this Advent season, either by yourself or with a group of family or friends, light a candle, and:

Reflect on the following:
1. How do you most see hope revealed in your life?
2. Is there someone in your life this season who needs hope? How can you share the hope that only comes from Jesus with him or her?

Pray:

Lord, thank you that you are my hope and my salvation. Whom shall I fear? Even if things are not how I would want them to be, I have hope in you. You are my rock and refuge. My help comes from you. May the hope I have in you be evident by the way I live and love people. May people not want my life or riches, but may they want the Jesus they see in me. In Jesus' name I pray, amen.

DAY FIFTEEN

HOPE FOR ALL PEOPLE

D O YOU REALIZE the promise of hope that has existed throughout time is the same today because of the person of Jesus Christ? Hope has never changed.

Even though Mary was not married, she received word from the angel Gabriel that she would become pregnant. She did not doubt the message, but instead asked Gabriel, "'How will this be since I am a virgin?'" (Luke 1:34). Mary's fiancé, Joseph, also received a visit from an angel. The angel told Joseph it was all going to be okay, he needed to marry Mary and she would give birth to a son who would save people from their sins (Matthew 1:20–21). The angel quoted directly from Isaiah 7:14:

"Therefore the Lord himself will give you a sign: The virgin will conceive and give birth to a son, and will call him Immanuel."

Do you know why Joseph went ahead and married Mary despite what people might say about his pregnant fiancée?

It was because both he and Mary knew God's promises. God chose them both to participate in His plan. According to the angel Gabriel, Mary was "highly favored" (Luke 1:28). Joseph came from the tribe of Judah. They both said *"Yes"* to God.

The shepherds who received word about the baby's birth found Mary and Joseph and told everyone what they had heard about the baby (Luke 2:16–18). I love Mary's response to everything she heard:

"Mary kept all these things in her heart and thought about them often." (Luke 2:19, NLT)

She kept the hope of the world in her heart and pondered the promises of God—she knew everything the shepherds said was true because the angel Gabriel had already told her. On that starry night, in a lowly stable, God delivered His promised hope to a broken world.

Do you know this hope? Do you keep God's promises in your heart and think about them often? **Hope** is our connection to heaven, and it came in the form of a precious baby. This season, make sure you know Him; hang on tight, and never let go.

DAY SIXTEEN

WITNESS TO HOPE

CAN'T TELL YOU how many times in one week I hear someone say, "Jesus, please come soon!" For those whose eternity is secure, we yearn for Jesus to come and rescue us once and for all from this broken world.

There was a man in Jerusalem named Simeon who was called "righteous and devout" (Luke 2:25). He was one of the remnants of Israel prophesied about in Isaiah 10:21–22. The Holy Spirit promised Simeon he would not die before he had a chance to see the Messiah (Luke 2:26). Because he was filled with the Holy Spirit, he was completely tuned in when the Holy Spirit told him to *"Go!"*

One day, because of his obedience to the prompting of the Holy Spirit, Simeon ended up at the Temple at the same time Mary and Joseph arrived to dedicate Jesus to the Lord and provide the purification offering (Luke 2:22–24). Upon seeing Jesus, Simeon took the baby in his arms and said:

Now Lord, you are releasing your bond-servant
to depart in peace, according to your word; for
my eyes have seen your salvation, which you
have prepared in the presence of all peoples, a
light of revelation to the Gentiles, and the glory
of your people Israel. (Luke 2:29–32)

Simeon had waited his whole life to see the promised
Messiah. He was a devout Jewish man who knew all about
the prophecies of the coming Messiah. Can you imagine his
expectant hope every day when he got out of bed? How many
times do you think he thought, *Today could be the day*?

I don't know about you, but I have not received confirmation from the Holy Spirit that I will witness the return of Jesus
in my lifetime—but, it doesn't matter. I will continue to wake
up with the same expectant **hope** Simeon had because God is
faithful, and regardless of whether Jesus comes back in my lifetime, He was and is to come. Just like Simeon, believers today
are filled with the Holy Spirit. We should be obedient to *"Go!"*
when told. You just never know what you might witness today.

DAY SEVENTEEN

JOY TO THE WORLD

W HAT COMES TO mind when you see these three words at
Christmas: love, joy, and peace? These words are every-
where. They are on decorations, flashing neon signs, tele-
vision commercials, and Christmas cards. These words look
great when everything is going well in your life, but what about
when things are not so great?

Retailers are pretty good at cashing in on themes from the
Bible. They did not come up with love, joy, and peace on their
own. We see these themes throughout the Bible, and in fact,
the angel announced to the shepherds that he was bringing
"good news that will cause great *joy* for all the people" (Luke
2:10, emphasis mine). The people would be joyful because a
baby born that day was the One who would save the world.
Who wouldn't want to be the bearer of good news like this?

Christmas is an excellent time to give gifts. It is always
better to give than to receive. However, when it comes to our

Christmas gift giving, sometimes we often overlook those who are downtrodden or a little grumpy. That is why I am glad God thought of me when He delivered His Christmas gift, because before I met Jesus, I was a bit downtrodden and grumpy. I desperately needed His gift.

There was someone in the Temple on the day of Jesus' dedication who needed a gift too. At the same time Simeon talked about Jesus with Mary and Joseph, a prophetess named Anna walked by. Anna had been a widow for more than eighty years. Sadly, she was only married to her husband for seven years before he died (Luke 2:36–37). Even though she was not living the dream, she was at the Temple "day and night worshipping God with fasting and prayer" (Luke 2:37, NLT). She was a faithful woman, and as soon as she heard Simeon, she praised God. She began to tell everyone near her what she had heard (Luke 2:38). She was full of excitement and joy.

Every day, many people cross our path—family members, friends, coworkers, neighbors, baristas, waiters—you name it. Some of them need hope, love, joy, and peace more than ever this season. Be the bearer of the Good News that will bring great **hope**, love, joy, and peace to their lives. It is a simple gift, and it won't cost you anything but your time and love for the world He came to save.

DAY EIGHTEEN

A SHINING STAR

IN THE SOUTH where I live, it is not unusual to see "Jesus is the Reason for the Season" on everything—yard signs, decorative plates, Christmas cards, banners, T-shirts, coffee cups—you name it. However, when I travel outside the South at Christmas, this is not always the case. Cities across America sparkle with bright lights, Santa, reindeers, hot chocolate, and shopping, but if you ask people, "What does Christmas mean to you?" the majority will not mention anything about Jesus. People throughout the years have had the opportunity to hear about the true Christmas story, yet they continue to miss it or ignore it.

A little more than two thousand years ago, this same thing happened. The wise men from the east arrived in Jerusalem and went around town asking the people, "Where is the one who has been born king of the Jews? We saw his star when it rose and have come to worship him" (Matthew 2:2). These wise men, or astrologers, were not God-fearing Jews. Scholars believe they may have been from Babylonia, where Jews were numerous. This might indicate why they were familiar with the reference to the star (Numbers 24:17). However, these wise men were Gentiles. King Herod heard what the wise men were saying, and he became deeply disturbed.

King Herod was wicked and insecure. He murdered two of his wives and three of his sons because he suspected them of plotting against him. You can only imagine what he felt when he heard these wise men announcing the birth of a new king. Herod gathered the leading priests and teachers of religious law and asked them, "Where is the Messiah supposed to be born?" (Matthew 2:4). They all answered, "Bethlehem," because that is what the prophet Micah said (Micah 5:2–4).

King Herod gathered the wise men to figure out when the star first appeared. After their meeting, Herod told them, "Go to Bethlehem and search carefully for the child. And when you find him, come back and tell me so that I can go and worship him too" (Matthew 2:8). Problem is, Herod wasn't being honest. Herod didn't want to worship the newborn king; he wanted to kill him. Did you notice anything else? The leading priests and teachers made no attempt to go and find the baby. None whatsoever.

Herod's wicked intent didn't stop God's plan. God set the star in the sky and led the wise men directly to Jesus (Matthew 2:9). When the star stopped, the Bible says the wise men rejoiced, entered the house, bowed down, worshiped Jesus, and gave him precious gifts (Matthew 2:10–11). Tradition says there were only three wise men, based on the number of gifts, but we don't know if this is correct. Imagine for a minute the possibility of a lot of wise men—Gentiles, mind you—being filled with joy, bowing and worshipping before Jesus, and presenting him with lots and lots of gifts.

Even though the wise men had seen the star rise, they went asking questions in the wrong city. Bethlehem was close to six miles south of Jerusalem. These wise men knew about the star, but they either didn't know or remember Micah had specifically said Bethlehem. King Herod didn't even have any wise men watching for the star—his wise men weren't that wise after all. We don't know exactly how long it took for the wise men to arrive in Jerusalem or how long they stayed, but some time had passed by the time they arrived in Bethlehem (my youngest son refused to put the wise men near our nativity scene this year because of this passage).

Mary, Joseph, and Jesus had already moved from the stable to a house. Once Herod figured out he had been tricked, he ordered all the boys who were two years old and younger in and around Bethlehem to be killed (Matthew 2:16).

The Gentile wise men met baby Jesus and worshiped Him. When it was time for them to return home, they went a different route to avoid King Herod. How did they know to do this? God warned them in a dream (Matthew 5:12). After their encounter with the Messiah, the wise men heard from God.

The wise men met the real meaning of Christmas that day they came upon Mary and Joseph's home. They reacted to the Savior. They surrendered (bowed), worshiped, and turned from their ways (by not going back to Jerusalem). We don't know what their lives looked like after this encounter in Bethlehem and how many, if any, Gentiles came to know Jesus because of it. Yet, one thing is for sure—they responded to the Savior.

Maybe you've spent your whole life celebrating Christmas, but you have missed the Savior. You've heard part of the Christmas story. Maybe you have even heard it all, but your eyes, your ears, and your heart have not been open to it—until now. Imagine for a moment following the star and finding the king baby. What would you have done or said?

Don't let this Christmas go by without bowing, worshipping, repenting, and accepting Him as Lord and Savior of your life. Have you personally responded to Jesus? There is no need to look for the star any longer. Jesus Christ was born, and He is the **hope** of the world.

DAY NINETEEN

HEAVEN KISSED THE EARTH

I REMEMBER HOLDING MY first child in my arms minutes after giving birth. So many thoughts swirled in my head. I had no idea if I was prepared to be a mom or knew what to do. Up until that moment, I had never held a newborn baby. It was a surreal moment, for sure. One minute, my son was tucked away nicely inside, and the next, he was placed in my arms for me to care for. The responsibility of it all was quite overwhelming and beautiful at the same time.

I can't even begin to imagine the thoughts racing through Mary's head the moment Jesus lay in her arms for the first time. She was in a dirty stable, in the cold and darkness, holding the One who would save the world. Mary stared into the face of God as she held baby Jesus close.

Heaven kissed the earth the moment Jesus was born. The Bible says:

"For God so loved the world that he gave his one and only Son, that whoever believes in him shall not perish but have eternal life." (John 3:16)

God's love came down in the form of a baby. It was yet another example of God's fulfillment of prophecy. The prophet Isaiah spoke these words close to seven hundred years before that special day:

> Here is my servant whom I have chosen, the one I love, in whom I delight; I will put my Spirit on him, and he will proclaim justice to the nations. He will not quarrel or cry out; no one will hear his voice in the streets. A bruised reed he will not break, and a smoldering wick he will not snuff out, till he has brought justice through to victory. In his name the nations will put their hope. (Matthew 12:18–21)

God sent His precious son to a broken world to give us **hope** in His name. Every problem, every crisis, every doubt, and every sin will be erased in the name of Jesus. The verse right after the well-known John 3:16 says, "For God did not send his Son into the world to condemn the world, but to save the world through him." In the past, because of their sins, God sent kings to destroy His people. However, this time God sent a new kind of king—a King of all kings—who would deliver, not destroy.

The name of Jesus is offensive to many in the world because they don't know the hope He offers. They've never received the best gift of all—the free gift of eternal life (Ephesians 2:8). As you look at your Christmas shopping list this season, are you praying the people on your list have (or receive) this gift? If they have never received it, pray God will give you an opportunity to share this gift with them this year.

DAY TWENTY

LIGHT OF THE WORLD

I GREW UP IN a church that lit an Advent wreath during Christmas. A different candle was lit each of the four Sundays leading up to Christmas, and a different Scripture was read each week. The candles represented the themes of the season: hope (or expectation), love, joy, and peace. The fifth candle, which was always white, stood in the middle of the evergreen wreath (the circle represented God's unending love). It was always lit on Christmas Eve. This candle stood as a reminder that Jesus is the light of the world. The Advent wreath is so simple yet packed with so much symbolism.

I was thinking about candles recently. Candlelight is so subtle. The light put off by a candle is never offensive, and never glaring. As beautiful as candlelight is, it can also be frustrating because the light from a candle only lights up a specific amount of space. If you are in a dark room and want to move about while only using a candle, you must carry the candle with you to light your path. You can't see too far ahead of you, and generally you can only see what is near you.

Humans cannot see in the darkness and therefore need light. God did not give us the unique ability to see in the dark. If we could see in the dark, the necessity for light might not be that important to us. Putting up lots of twinkle lights at Christmas makes this season look pretty and festive, but these temporary lights burn out and are packed away shortly after Christmas. Candles burn only until the wick runs out. Man-made light never lasts forever. How can we be guaranteed to always have access to a light source? Stay close to Jesus.

Jesus made a bold statement to a group of people in the Treasury in the Temple. Jesus often chose to address people in the Treasury located in the section of the Temple called the Court of the Women so both men and women could hear what He had to say. He said, "I am the light of the world. Whoever follows me will never walk in darkness, but will have the light of life" (John 8:12). Daniel said God knows what is hidden in the darkness even though He is surrounded by light (Daniel 2:22).

We have a limited scope of sight, but He has an unlimited view. We cannot simply gaze at His light. Jesus said we must follow Him because He is the Light. He lights our path just enough according to His enough. The psalmist said in Psalm 147:11, "The Lord delights in those who fear him, who put their hope in his unfailing love." The Lord gives favor to those who trust in Him by promising they will never walk in darkness and guarantees the light of eternal life. His Light will never burn out.

As Christians, we carry His light within us. Believers have the responsibility to be a conduit of Jesus' light in this world (Matthew 5:16). Is your light burning brightly for Jesus this season? Regardless of whether your church does an Advent wreath or not, perhaps this year is the year you need to start one at home. It's not too late to start. We can stare at the darkness and do nothing, or we can choose to light a candle in the dark. The Light of the world stepped down into darkness to overcome the darkness. May He illuminate all that is around you so you can see His love and the **hope** the world has because of Him.

DAY TWENTY-ONE

HOPE DEFINED

What is hope?

Hope

Noun

- a feeling of expectation and desire for a certain thing to happen.
- a person or thing that may help or save someone.
- a feeling of trust.

Verb

- to want something to happen or be the case.[3]

'M SURE WE can all agree we hope for different things in our lifetime. As kids, we hope we get the gifts on our Christmas

---

[3] "Hope", Dictionary.com. Accessed June 07, 2017, http://www.dictionary.com/browse/hope?s=t.

list, and we hope Christmas break comes quickly. Some hope for Christmas vacations filled with skiing or trips to the beach. The list gets added to as the years go by. We hope for so many things, and often-answered hopes start to go unnoticed because they become expected or mundane. Sometimes we even take the things that were once "hopes" for granted.

What is the purpose for hope, and why does it matter when hope begins to fade? Sarah Young, in her devotional *Jesus Calling,* says, "Hope is a golden cord connecting you to heaven. Without the cord of hope, your head may slump and your feet may shuffle as you journey uphill with me."[4]

How can we share hope to someone whose head is slumping or maybe doesn't even know *the* hope? Dispensing hope in this world means so many different things. Some people give hope in the form of a handout. This kind of hope quickly fades once the handout goes away. The only thing that can be hoped for is the next handout. Doctors give out hope disguised as medicine, but what happens when the medicine fails to work? Hope quickly fades, and fear sets in. What happens when we combine practical things with spiritual things? We get the hope Sarah Young refers to as "the golden cord that connects us to Heaven."

Hebrews 11:1 uses the word *hope* to define faith:

"Now faith is the assurance of things hoped for, the conviction of things not seen."

---

[4] Sarah Young, *Jesus calling: seeking peace in His presence: devotions for every day of the year* (Nashville: **Integrity Publishers, 2004), 218.**

Depending on the version of the Bible you read, the word *hope* appears between one hundred and twenty- five and one hundred and seventy-five times. The word appears both in the Old and New Testament. Biblical hope covers all three aspects of dictionary.com's noun definition.

- We hope in the things God has promised in His Word.
- We must put our hope in Jesus as the One, and only One, who was sent to save us.
- We must put our trust in the Lord.

Look at David's hope found in the Psalms. He held on to this golden cord of hope.

Psalm 31:24 – "Be strong and take heart, all you who hope in the Lord."

Psalm 33:20 – "We wait in hope for the Lord; he is our help and our shield."

Psalm 33:22 – "May your unfailing love rest upon us, O Lord, even as we put our hope in you."

Psalm 39:7 – "But now, Lord, what do I look for? My hope is in you."

Psalm 42:11 – "Why are you downcast, O my soul? Why so disturbed within me? Put your hope in God, for I will yet praise him, my Savior and my God."

We can have little but have more hope than someone who has everything—it all depends on where our hope comes from, and what or in whom we are putting our faith. God-given hope allows us to keep our spirits up. It makes it possible to see and move in ways we never imagined possible. Hope is a lifeline. Hope is so much more than a wish because hope is always attainable because of Jesus.

Be a partaker of the hope God wants to give you. If you are lacking in hope right now, pray and seek Him about it. Surround yourself this season with people who are living hope-filled lives. **Hope** is a gift to be treasured and cherished, not just at Christmas, but all year.

REVELATION

A S YOU START out each week this Advent season, either by yourself or with a group of family or friends, light a candle, and:

Reflect on the following:

1. In what ways has Jesus revealed Himself to you?
2. What is it that you hope to still learn about Jesus? How will you discover more about Him?

Pray:

Jesus, you reveal yourself in marvelous ways. You have existed throughout time, and your name has been woven throughout history. Help me to draw closer to you this season by giving me the desire and the time to dig deeper into your Word so I can know you better. In Jesus' name I pray, amen.

DAY TWENTY-TWO

HIS REVELATION

ISN'T IT A great feeling when you finally figure something out? The "aha" moment can answer so many questions. God desires for each of us to have moments where we discover more and more about Him.

All people have access to God's goodness and His general revelation. In His kindness, God allows us to witness His creation. We get to enjoy beautiful sunsets and sunrises. We get to witness the change of seasons. We get to witness the complexity of the oceans, and marvel at mountains and valleys. We don't have to do anything to participate in His general revelation. His Creation exists all around us regardless of what you or I do. General revelation is the basis of our moral law, but it has no redemptive component. It in no way communicates the Gospel.

"For since the creation of the world God's invisible qualities—his eternal power and divine nature—have been clearly seen, being understood from what has been made, so that people are without excuse." (Romans 1:20)

However, God's special revelation is a whole different kind of revelation. Unlike general revelation, special revelation is the way in which God communicates His redemptive will for mankind. Special revelation is revealed through the Word, and through the person of Jesus Christ. One of the ways in which the authors of Scripture received special revelation was through theophanies. A *theophany* is a tangible manifestation of God. In most cases, it was a visible appearance of God.

The redemptive plan of God was woven throughout Scripture from the minute He approached Adam and Eve in the garden after they had sinned. He appeared. He didn't just destroy them (Genesis 3:8). God appeared several times to Abraham (Genesis 12:7–9, 17:1, 18:1). God appeared to Jacob at Bethel (Genesis 28:11–19). God appeared to Moses on the mountain (Exodus 19:20, 33:18–34:8), and in the transfer of leadership to Joshua (Deuteronomy 31:15). These are just a few examples of "the Lord coming down." All these "coming down" examples set the stage for the moment Jesus came down to earth.

God's Word is packed full of God's special revelation. The authors of Scripture, inspired by the Holy Spirit, recorded all God chose to communicate to us. God revealed Himself, His purpose, and His perfect timing.

And how from childhood you have known the sacred writings that are able to instruct you for salvation through faith in Christ Jesus. All Scripture is inspired by God and is useful for teaching, for reproof, for correction, and for training in righteousness, so that everyone who belongs to God may be proficient, equipped for every good work. (2 Timothy 3:15–17)

Through the prophets, God promised a Savior. That promise was kept. God has also promised His Son would come again. As we celebrate this Christmas season, we can enjoy the general revelation of the season in all its beauty. We also need to look to God's Word to meditate on the special revelation of the second coming of Christ. God reveals what we need to know about Him through the reading of Scripture. If we don't read it, we won't know.

As we enter this last week before Christmas, find moments to simplify. Maybe this means saying *"No"* to attending one more Christmas party. Maybe it means getting up a little earlier so you can spend time digging into the Scriptures we'll discuss this week about Jesus' second coming. Whatever it is for you, don't let this Advent pass without experiencing something special. The realization and **revelation** of Jesus' second coming should inspire you to prepare yourself and share the true meaning of Christmas with those you know and love. Make this a priority this year as you simplify your season.

DAY TWENTY-THREE

JOIN WITH THE ANGELS

WITHIN THE LAST twenty-four hours, I've heard two different pastors at two different churches preach on the same text. Some might say it's no coincidence, because it is, after all, the Christmas season. The text taught is one of the most popular Bible verses during the Christmas season. I, however, believe the Spirit is telling me—and now you—to be careful who and what we worship this Christmas season.

In my efforts to combat the spirit of busyness during Christmas, I must also combat the spirit of laziness. It's a fine balance not to overdo things without risking never doing any-thing. I refuse to overexert myself during Christmas. There are so many things I could add to my schedule, but I can't. I know myself well enough to know I will physically and emotionally wear myself out and I will not be able to serve my family well (my full-time job) or have any energy to worship my Savior. I also know if I'm not careful with my schedule, I will resent the

Christmas season altogether. I can't let that happen, because the season is about so much more than all the stuff we try to cram into it.

Today, these thoughts got me thinking, *Do we worship the season or do we worship the Savior?* If everything you know today, as it relates to Christmas, were stripped away, would you still love this season? To what, or whom, is your worship directed?

For thirty or so days, our lives are altered. We address Christmas cards, stand in long lines at the post office, shop online, go to the mall, attend Christmas parties, change up our corporate worship services, participate in or attend Christmas programs and pageants at school or church, wrap presents, decorate our houses, travel to family or have houseguests, and make holiday meals and desserts. Sometimes our job duties suffer a little this time of year. The chores around the house may or may not get done in a timely fashion. Drive-through dinners become the norm. Depending on where you live, the temperatures can drop, and so does church attendance. Our tiredness necessitates a "sleep-in Sunday." If we are not careful, a season to celebrate the birth of Jesus becomes so little about Jesus. Christmas itself all-too-often becomes an idol.

This is where worship comes in. God-centered worship rescues us from gods trying to keep us from Jesus. No matter what we are doing, what time of the year it is, or what we are going through, if we will turn to worshipping God in everything we do, it always reminds us that everything is about Him.

The shepherds were doing their job and minding their business the night Jesus was born. They were in fields nearby tending their sheep. An angel appeared to them and delivered the message about the Savior being born (Luke 2:8–12). Only one angel originally appeared to the shepherds. However, upon the announcement, the Bible says, "Suddenly a great company of the heavenly host appeared with the angel" (Luke 2:13). Upon the announcement of the newborn King, the angels left whatever they were doing and immediately went to worship Jesus. Scripture says the angels were "praising God and saying, 'Glory to God in the highest heaven, and on earth peace to those on whom his favor rests'" (Luke 2:13–14).

The angels didn't remain forever because Luke 2:15 says the angels returned to heaven. The angels responded in action and worship when they appeared. The shepherds also responded in action and worship. They said, "Let's go to Bethlehem and see this thing that has happened, which the Lord has told us about." When they saw the baby with their own eyes, they shared with everyone what the angel had told them (Luke 2:16–18). Even though the shepherds had to go back to their work, they "returned, glorifying and praising God for all the things they had heard and seen, which were just as they had been told" (Luke 2:20).

The shepherds were busy doing what they were called to do. The angels were busy doing what they do. The **revelation** of the person of Jesus Christ moved them to worship amidst their calling. They didn't just worship Him for a moment, a day, or a season; they continued in worship. They didn't worship the day, the birth, or the memories of that day; they worshiped God.

So, I return to my question, *Are you worshipping the season or are you worshipping Jesus?* If the season were truly simplified—no lights, no parties, no gifts—would it still be the most wonderful time of the year for you? Are busyness and the noise around you so much this season that you wouldn't notice if an angel appeared to you?

Focus your attention on a lifestyle of worship. Doing this will keep your eyes on Jesus, and much less on the worldly things fighting for your attention and energy.

DAY TWENTY-FOUR

GIFTS FOR THE KING

I'VE HEARD THE Christmas story my entire life, but I heard something the other day I had never heard or thought about before. I wrote the other day about the wise men from the East. They followed the star all the way to the Christ child in Bethlehem. They found Mary with Jesus, bowed down, and worshiped Him. Then they opened their treasure chests and gave Him gifts of gold, frankincense, and myrrh (Matthew 2:11). Why these gifts?

What I learned the other day was the gifts given by the wise men that day funded Joseph, Mary, and Jesus' escape to Egypt. My whole life, I've never heard this or thought about it in these terms, but it makes total sense. Joseph and Mary were young and had nothing. They were about to be forced to go to Egypt to save their lives, and they would have needed provisions. God provided a way. Not only were these gifts practical, they also represented the deity (gold), priesthood (frankincense), and future death (myrrh) of Jesus. These gifts given by the wise men confirmed, yet again, that Jesus was the Messiah, the one whom the prophets foretold.

These gifts were used to pay respect to the King of kings. They would also be used to pay his way. The wise men opened their chests and presented Jesus with their wealth. These riches would pay Joseph and Mary's debt just as Jesus would ultimately pay for our debts (our sins). Jesus, just thirty-three years later, would open His treasures and pour out His offering on the Cross.

His death on the Cross was a small revelation of what is to come for the believer. Daniel, in his vision, saw the final kingdom with the final ruler.

"Then the sovereignty, power and greatness of all the king-doms under heaven will be handed over to the holy people of the Most High. His kingdom will be an everlasting kingdom, and all rulers will worship and obey him." (Daniel 7:37)

John wrote about his vision in the book of Revelation. In Revelation 3:21, it says, "To the one who is victorious, I will give the right to sit with me on my throne, just as I was victo-rious and sat down with my Father on his throne." Our provi-sion has already been taken care of, but we need to be good stewards of this provision.

God didn't have to provide these gifts to Joseph, Mary, and Jesus. He could have taken care of their costs in another way. He also didn't have to confirm Jesus' deity. He chose to. Even though God provided, Joseph and Mary needed to move forward in obedience, heed the warning to flee to Egypt, and hide these things in their hearts. We need to do the same.

God provided the gift of salvation to us through the person of Jesus Christ. Jesus is our provision. He paid for our sins once and for all. He proved His deity by defeating the grave and being raised from the dead. As we wait for His Advent, we wait patiently and faithfully in the **revelation** of what is still to come. Jesus, who had no room for Him to be born in, has gone ahead of you and me to prepare a room for us in His Father's house (John 14:2). All of those who believe in Jesus Christ as their savior will enjoy treasures for eternity, and will be in the presence of Jesus forever.

The gifts given to Jesus by the wise men, though valuable and meant for royalty, didn't last forever. The gold would be used or traded. The frankincense would be burned as incense for offerings, and the myrrh would be used for ointments. The wise men's gifts weren't what you or I would give a new mother, but they were exactly what Mary needed at the time.

This season, are you giving gifts that have meaningful value, or are your gifts keeping up with the latest trends? Will people remember your gifts in a week or two? Are you opening and giving your treasures to those in need? Most importantly, are you sharing the greatest gift of all—the gift wrapped in the Gospel?

DAY TWENTY-FIVE

PEACE ON EARTH

A COUPLE SUMMERS AGO, we, along with some friends of ours, went to Disney World. The first time we walked into the Magic Kingdom, I said to my friend, "It is so surreal in here. There is so much chaos going on in the world, but in here it is as if time is standing still." This morning as I sit in the quiet of my home in the glow of Christmas tree lights, this same thought struck me again.

Turn on the news or read the newspaper, and you will find that the world is full of chaos, uncertainty, and fear. Just as I felt a twinge of guilt in the Magic Kingdom, I feel that same twinge of guilt every Christmas because I know there are many in the world struggling. I know some children won't receive a single gift. I know people are living in war-torn countries, cold, and displaced. I know people are struggling with severe depression. I know many will die of heart attacks, cancer, and sickness this season. Just a few years ago, my grandfather passed away quietly on Christmas Day.

Yet...

"Glory to God in the highest heaven, and on earth peace to those on whom his favor rests." (Luke 2:13–14)

Amidst the struggle, chaos, and noise of the world, the peace the angels spoke about is possible. "Peace on Earth" is the tagline on our family Christmas card this year. It is what we sing at Christmas time. However, the world doesn't just stand still during Christmas. As much as we want to hide in our Christmas bubbles, bad things still happen during the Christmas season. How do we balance the joy of the season with the hard stuff in the world?

The answer is Jesus.

"I have told you these things, so that in me you may have peace. In this world you will have trouble. But take heart! I have overcome the world." (John 16:33)

Jesus said we would have trouble in this world. So how then is peace on earth possible? Our peace comes from Him. Without Jesus, and the fruit of the Holy Spirit, we will struggle with finding peace on this earth. Before I received a **revelation** of my need for a personal relationship with Jesus Christ, peace was the thing I lacked most. Yet, the moment I surrendered my life to Him, a peace washed over me that has never left.

"Peace I leave with you; my peace I give you. I do not give to you as the world gives. Do not let your hearts be troubled and do not be afraid." (John 14:27)

Jesus knew it would be hard for us to live in this world. Our hearts long for perfect peace because we long for Him. The quietness of my home will end as my family awakes from their slumber. The soft light coming from the lights of my Christmas tree will be overtaken by the sunlight and all the other light sources in my home. However, as things in my environment change, this peace-filled quiet doesn't have to leave my soul. My slice of peace on earth is in me because He is in me.

His peace doesn't make us apathetic to the hard things of this world. A life lived with Jesus at the center gives us a peace that surpasses all understanding (Philippians 4:7)—even when we struggle to understand the hard things. If peace is the gift you desire most this year, the Bible tells us we must "seek peace and pursue it" (1 Peter 3:11). Seek Jesus. Ask Him to reveal Himself to you in a personal way so you can be at peace on this earth this season and all year.

DAY TWENTY-SIX

FULL OF LIFE

A S I OPENED Christmas cards this afternoon, a Scripture reference inside one of the cards caught my eye. It wasn't one I see that often on Christmas cards. It made me chuckle because I had already been thinking about what I was going to write for today.

"I have come that they may have life, and have it to the full." (John 10:10)

How full has your life been this season?

In our affluent culture, we fill our lives with many things. We have big houses, big cars, second houses, and storage units to hold what we can't fit inside our large homes. We fill our schedules with work, physical exercise, lunches, dinners, movies, carpool, sporting events, concerts, church, and the list could go on and on. We fill and fill, and there is no better time than Christmas to see how much we can overfill our schedules, our waistlines, and our shopping carts. Was Jesus referring to this kind of "full" when He said these words?

No, He wasn't. The word "full" in this context means over and above, exceedingly abundantly, more remarkable, and much more than all. Jesus said these words after saying He was the gate people needed to enter through, and that the thief comes only to steal, kill, and destroy (John 10:9–10). Jesus didn't refer to stuff in this life; He referred to our eternal life. He referred to our souls.

We are twenty-six days into Advent. I am not sure if you have had the opportunity to simplify your season. Maybe you just haven't been able to pull it off yet. Please don't give up. There are still a few more days before Christmas, and every minute counts. There is still time to have a simple and full Christmas even if that means everything isn't perfect and every gift hasn't been purchased or wrapped.

In Revelation 7:16–17, John heard:

> Never again will they hunger; never again will they thirst. The sun will not beat down on them, nor any scorching heat. For the Lamb at the center of the throne will be their shepherd; he will lead them to springs of living water. And God will wipe away every tear from their eyes.

This is the full life to which Jesus referred. We have far more because of Him. Jesus isn't a Scrooge, but we must remember it wasn't Jesus who invented our modern concept of Christmas. Living simply here on earth means to put Jesus at the center of everything. When we do that, our perspective changes.

DAY TWENTY-SEVEN

TIME OF HIS RETURN

S A YOUNG girl, I went to the midnight service on Christmas Eve. By the end of the service, I was always ready to get home because I thought if I wasn't home and fast asleep, Santa would pass my house. I had butterflies in my stomach the entire night. After a few hours of sleep, I hurried down the stairs to see the presents under the tree. As I got older, I realized Santa wasn't the one leaving the presents, and when I went to bed on Christmas Eve, I no longer had butterflies in my stomach. Instead, I longed for sleep. Now that I have children of my own, I've witnessed the anticipation of Christmas again through their eyes.

Even though they are past their Santa days, their anticipation this year has me thinking. *Have the butterflies left us as we continue to wait for Jesus' second coming?* We've waited and waited, but no matter how bad things get, He still hasn't returned. Has our hope faded? I hope not. We have God's special **revelation** that Jesus is coming again.

> But about that day or hour no one knows, not even the angels in heaven, nor the Son, but only the Father. As it was in the days of Noah, so it will be at the coming of the Son of Man. For in the days before the flood, people were eating and drinking, marrying and giving in marriage, up to the day Noah entered the ark; and they knew nothing about what would happen until the flood came and took them all away. That is how it will be at the coming of the Son of Man. (Matthew 24:36–39)

As children, we all knew the day Santa would travel around the world to deliver presents. We listened for reindeer hooves on the rooftop, a jolly laugh, or a "Ho-Ho-Ho." On Christmas morning, the evidence of his coming would lie around the bottom of the Christmas tree.

Even though we don't know the exact date or time Jesus will return, it doesn't mean He's never coming. We have proof in the Bible that Jesus' first arrival was spoken of through the prophets. We have historical evidence Jesus existed. Now we must cling to the hope that just as the words about Jesus' birth were fulfilled, His second coming will also be fulfilled.

As we prepare ourselves to celebrate Christmas with our families and friends, we must be mindful of continuing to prepare ourselves for His second coming. Even at this moment, God is working out His plan. We cannot be preoccupied with life's festivities, and ignore His warnings. Our minds and hearts need to be set on Jesus every single day of the year because this is what Jesus told us to do.

> Therefore keep watch, because you do not know on what day your Lord will come. But understand this: If the owner of the house had known at what time of night the thief was coming, he would have kept watch and would not have let his house be broken into. So you also must be ready, because the Son of Man will come at an hour when you do not expect him. (Matthew 24:42–44)

DAY TWENTY-EIGHT

A SAVIOR IS BORN

ODAY, THE LAST day of Advent, is the day people will gather in churches around the world to celebrate the birth of Jesus Christ. Many churches will light the final Advent candle today—the white candle in the center of the Advent wreath remembering Jesus as the light of the world. People will lift up the name of Jesus as they sing carols, and prepare their hearts to hear the Christmas story once again. These words will be heard over and over, "She gave birth to her firstborn, a son. She wrapped him in cloths and placed him in a manger, because there was no guest room available for them" (Luke 2:7).

Joseph and Mary traveled from Nazareth to Bethlehem to fulfill Joseph's obligation to register in the census called by the Roman Emperor Augustus.

> And everyone went to their own town to register. So Joseph also went up from the town

of Nazareth in Galilee to Judea, to Bethlehem
the town of David, because he belonged to the
house and line of David. He went there to register with Mary, who was pledged to be married
to him and was expecting a child. (Luke 2:3–5)

Not only had they traveled, but many others did as well.
The small town of Bethlehem was full of travelers. Scripture
says there was no room for Joseph and Mary—no one would
receive them. Did Joseph have no extended family left in
Bethlehem? Did no one care about this pregnant girl? The only
accommodations they could find were in a place where animals were housed. A frantic first-time father surely would have
let people know his wife was about to give birth.

No one made room for Joseph or Mary. They made no
room for Jesus.

Charles Spurgeon once reflected on why Jesus had to be
born in a stable. He said, "We might tremble to approach a
throne, but we cannot fear to approach a manger." Jesus' birth
in the free stable reflected the humiliation he would suffer, and
the fact Jesus is free to all people. Would the shepherds have
approached Jesus had he been born anywhere else?

Churches today are the stables—a free place where *all*
can come and hear the Gospel message. On this final day of
Advent, may many prepare room in their hearts to receive
Jesus as their Lord and Savior. As little Christs, may we reflect
the humble spirit of Jesus through the power of the Holy Spirit,

and may our churches be lighthouses ready to receive all the weary travelers in need (the same is true of our homes and Christmas dinner tables). May today and tomorrow simply be filled with reflecting on the overwhelming love of the Father who sent His Son for you.

I hope you have discovered more about who Christ is to you this Advent season. Merry Christmas Eve!

EPIPHANY

IN CASE YOU need an excuse to leave your Christmas decor up a little longer, I want to share this nugget with you.

Epiphany isn't new to me. I grew up in a church that recognized Epiphany. I remember the liturgical readings during the season, the different-colored robes the pastors wore, and the songs we sang. However, I never truly understood what Epiphany meant. I am not sure if I just missed it as a child/youth because I wasn't paying attention, or perhaps like many things within the church, we fail to explain things because we think everyone already knows.

One of the definitions of "epiphany" is, "A sudden realization about the nature or meaning of something."[5] As is the case many times for me, I had an epiphany about Epiphany the other night while sitting in a room of kindergartners through fourth graders. Jesus had it right when He said we need to

---

[5] "Epiphany", Dictionary.com. Accessed June 11, 2017, http://www. dictionary.com/browse/epiphany?s=t.

become like little children to understand things at times (Matthew 18:3).

We learned that historical accounts point to Epiphany as the celebration *after* Jesus' birth. It started on December 25 and ended with a festival on January 6. This blows the theory of Santa showing up on December 25 because, in many cultures, gifts are given on January 6. Our ancestors knew how to stretch out celebrations. We, on the other hand, run ourselves ragged leading up to major celebrations (such as celebrating Jesus' birthday), and within a few short minutes, the gifts are frantically unwrapped and the moment is over.

We also learned the other night about the possibility that the well-known song "The Twelve Days of Christmas" represented a much more Christian tradition than the mostly secularized tradition it holds today.[6] As you research this for yourself, I hope the meaning behind it gets stuck in your head as much as the tune will.

Savor what these seasons of Advent and Epiphany are all about—a gift sent by God to save you from eternal separation from Him (John 3:16). A priceless gift, indeed.

---

[6] Edwin And Jennifer Woodruff Tait, "The Real 12 Days of Christmas". Christian History | Learn the History of Christianity & the Church. Accessed June 11, 2017, http://www.christianitytoday.com/history/2008/august/real-twelve-days-of-christmas.html.

ABOUT THE AUTHOR

ERIN OLSON'S PRIMARY job as a homemaker consists of serving her husband, Scott, her three children, and three Havanese pups. She volunteers in the women and children's ministries, teaches Bible study, and is the director of a Bible fellowship class at her church. She also leads a women's Bible study in her neighborhood. She is a conference and luncheon speaker for groups ranging from students to senior adults. There are many ministries, missionaries, and children in the United States and around the world that have a piece of her heart and support.

Erin launched her blog, *Sandalfeet Ministries*, in January 2012 (sandalfeet.org). She is also a contributing writer on several Christian blogs. Erin is the author of two books: a 10-week Bible study, *Forgiveness - Unforgiveness: Revealed Through Your Fruits* and a devotional, *Sit at His Feet: Choose What is Better*. She has several more books in the works. In addition to her writing, Erin has a ministry podcast available on iTunes (*Sandalfeet Ministries*).

Before staying at home with her children, Erin worked as a corporate/intellectual property paralegal for large firms and corporations for close to a decade.

Erin has a Bachelor's Degree in Business Administration from Regis University (Denver, Colorado) and a Master's Degree in Christian Leadership from Liberty Baptist Theological Seminary (Lynchburg, Virginia). She is an ordained minister. Erin and her family reside in Dallas, Texas.